Great Ex~

Text by Eric Tomb

Drawings by Nancy Conkle

The King of Portugal after Waldseemüller's *Carta Marina*, 1516

The embellishments following are from the ancient maps of Waghenaer, Plancius, Hondius, Bleau, Ortelius, De Bry, *et al.*, and the heraldic arms of the explorers are from manuscripts in the great libraries of Spain and Portugal, *etc.*

The World in 1400

There had been a time when the great cultures of Europe and Asia communicated with one another. Merchants travelled between Greece and India; for a few short years, the Empire of Alexander the Great actually contained some of both countries. The Han Dynasty of China had regular trade relations and even exchanged a few diplomats with the Roman Empire.

Then, in the fourth and fifth centuries A.D., hordes of barbarians overran China, India and Europe, devastating their economies and disrupting trade between them. Just as Europe was beginning to re-form, the new religion of Islam engulfed North Africa and the Eastern Mediterranean, and reached into Spain and France. The enduring hostility between the Christian kingdoms of Europe and their Muslim neighbors cut Europeans off from the trade routes to the East. The Crusaders, who temporarily recaptured some of the Eastern Mediterranean during the twelfth century, had barely whetted their appetite for Asian luxuries when they were ejected. Some decided trade was more important than religion.

The Italians were in the best position (the middle of the Mediterranean) to act as intermediaries with the Muslims; Genoa and Venice became the most powerful of the Italian trading cities, with mighty navies and colonies around the Mediterranean; in the end Venice became the stronger of the two, the wealthiest city in Europe.

The Lion of Saint Mark, the emblem of Venice

A great opportunity arose in the thirteenth century, when the nomadic Mongols conquered most of Eurasia, from Korea to Hungary to Palestine. For the first time in centuries, a merchant could travel unmolested from Europe to China. Two Venetians, Niccoló and Maffeo Polo, first made this journey almost by accident, but when they learned how interested the Mongol Emperor Kublai Khan was in foreign cultures, they tried to recruit other Europeans to return with them. Niccoló's seventeen-year-old son Marco was the only one to complete the four-year journey back across Central Asia to China with them, but he so impressed Kublai Khan that he stayed in his service for seventeen years.

Marco Polo's description of his travels, written while he was a prisoner-of-war in Genoa, gave Europe its first picture of the wonders of Asia. The route across Central Asia closed again soon afterwards with the collapse of the Mongol Empire. But by then Europeans had been so aroused by Marco Polo's accounts — and by the legend of a mighty Christian king called Prester John, who ruled somewhere in Asia or Africa — that they were determined to find a direct route of their own to the riches of the East.

Marco Polo from
the first printed
edition, Nuremburg,
1477

Prince Henry the Navigator

1394-1460

Portugal was a small and out-of-the-way country; it seemed unlikely to have much influence on European affairs. But although King João I had brought peace and some prosperity to his land, his young sons (who had an English mother, Philippa of Lancaster) needed an outlet for their energy. The tasks they chose changed forever the way Europeans dealt with the rest of the world.

It was the third son, Henry, who provided the inspiration. The Portuguese had driven the Muslim Moors out of their country a century before; now the seventeen-year-old Henry suggested that they attack the Moorish city of Ceuta (just across from Gibraltar in North Africa). The brothers planned the expedition for four years; in 1415, they captured Ceuta after a single day's skirmishing.

The brothers returned to Portugal, but Henry remained fascinated with Africa. He returned to defend Ceuta a few years later, and tried in vain to capture Tangier, another Moorish city. He then retired to the southwestern corner of Portugal and devoted himself to geography and seamanship. At Sagres, the "sacred promontory" jutting out into the Atlantic, he assembled some of the finest astronomers and mapmakers of the day. Comparing their theories with the reports brought in by sailors, he began a truly systematic study of navigation and mapping.

Royal Arms of Portugal

There was a practical purpose to all this effort. Henry wanted to outflank the Moors, find the legendary Christian king Prester John, and maybe discover a little gold. From 1419 until his death, he sent expedition after expedition down the Atlantic coast of Africa. Although he never went along himself, his men settled the Azores, Madeira and Cape Verde islands and slowly uncovered the secrets of coastal Africa. Perhaps because of an ancient tradition that the ocean was boiling near the Equator, they moved very cautiously toward it at first; it was forty years before Pedro de Sintra reached Sierra Leone, a third of the way down the coast. But Bartholomeu Dias became the first European to round the Cape of Good Hope, only twenty-seven years after Henry's death.

The African expeditions led to a boom in trade and the Portuguese began to treat Henry's discoveries as state secrets (some say these included reaching America in the 1480s). But Henry's greatest contribution to navigation was too useful to keep hidden. The caravels his shipbuilders developed were much smaller and easier to handle than Mediterranean trading ships; they became the standard exploring ships for the next century.

Vasco da Gama

c. 1469-1524

"Let us hear no more of Ulysses and Aeneas and their long journeys, no more of Alexander and Trajan and their famous victories. My theme is the courage and fame of the Portuguese, to whom both Neptune and Mars pay homage. The ancient poets and heroes have had their day; a new and higher idea of valor has arisen." In the first lines of his poem *The Lusiads*, the Portuguese poet Camoens announces that he will write a great epic based not on ancient myths but on the explorers who made their way from Portugal to India. In a book with many heroes, the greatest of all is Vasco da Gama.

In Camoens's poem, the gods Jupiter, Mars and Venus help Da Gama, while Bacchus tries to keep him from reaching India. But the real Da Gama had enough obstacles in his world to overcome. Although the Portuguese had eighty years experience sailing down the coast of Africa and Da Gama himself had won a high reputation as a sailor and diplomat, the voyage he began in July, 1497, may have been the most daring venture any European mariner had ever undertaken. Portuguese explorers up to and including Bartholomeu Dias had stayed close to the African coast. Da Gama took his four ships (with some 170 men) far out into the Atlantic to find the best winds and currents, and his fleet was out of sight of land for over thirteen weeks. But his navigation was so good that he saw land again only 125 miles north of the Cape of Good Hope. Still, thirty men had died of scurvy by the time he had rounded the Cape and reached Mozambique.

Arms of Vasco da Gama

The East African ports were all ruled by Muslims and Da Gama had to move very cautiously to avoid trouble; in Mombasa his fleet barely escaped a Muslim attack. But in Malindi he somehow managed to get Ahmad ibn-Majid, the greatest Muslim navigator of the day, to guide him to India. Arriving in Calicut, he had to soothe the suspicions of the Hindu ruler and defuse the hostility of the Muslim traders. He did little trading in India and lost thirty more men to scurvy on his return trip, but he was a national hero when he reached Lisbon in September, 1499.

He returned to India as a conqueror. A second Portuguese expedition there had been a failure, so Da Gama was dispatched with twenty ships in 1502. He bombarded Calicut, destroyed Muslim shipping and established Portuguese trading posts along the coast. This time he arrived home laden with booty, prepared to retire in comfort. He was recalled a third time to become Viceroy of India in 1524, but died shortly after taking up his post.

Arms of Da Gama surmounted by the king to honor the great admiral

Vasco da Gama after Gaspar Correia

Christopher Columbus

c. 1451-1506

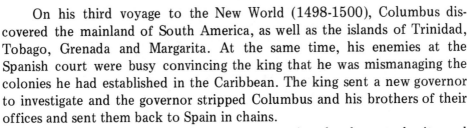

The Royal Arms of Spain

The Arms of Granada

On his third voyage to the New World (1498-1500), Columbus discovered the mainland of South America, as well as the islands of Trinidad, Tobago, Grenada and Margarita. At the same time, his enemies at the Spanish court were busy convincing the king that he was mismanaging the colonies he had established in the Caribbean. The king sent a new governor to investigate and the governor stripped Columbus and his brothers of their offices and sent them back to Spain in chains.

The captain of the ship that was transporting the three took pity and offered to remove their chains. With the stubbornness and self-assurance that had always marked his career, Columbus turned him down: he was waiting to be vindicated by the king and queen. Soon enough he was. His property was restored, he was compensated for his tribulations, and the governor was summarily dismissed. With a newly outfitted fleet, he set out on his fourth and last voyage of discovery, this time without any administrative duties.

It was this kind of determination that had made Columbus what he was, the discoverer of the New World. He was born in Genoa, Italy, the son of a weaver, and first went to sea when he was fourteen. Although he tried various studies and trades on land, he took increasingly to sailing, travelling throughout the Mediterranean and possibly as far as Iceland in the North Atlantic. Around 1478, he settled in Portugal, where he married a woman of high rank and set himself up as a mapmaker.

The idea that the world was round and that it might be possible to reach the Orient by sailing West was very much talked about at that time. But most geographers thought that the Atlantic Ocean must be too wide to be easily navigable. A westward crossing was theoretically interesting, but nothing more. Columbus was doing his own calculations, however; from his studies of Marco Polo and other writers and his discussions with various cartographers, he concluded that Japan must be about 2500 miles west of the Canary Islands. Once he decided that the voyage was possible, he determined to be the one to make it.

For nearly a decade, Columbus approached the kings of Portugal, Spain, England and France (especially the first two) for support. Most men might have despaired after half a dozen rejections, but Columbus persevered until King Ferdinand and Queen Isabella of Spain, who in 1492 finally succeeded in expelling the Moors from Granada, reconsidered and approved the project.

The famous voyage of the *Niña*, the *Pinta* and the *Santa María* (Columbus's flagship) began on August 3, 1492. In spite of fair following winds for most of the journey, it lasted far longer than Columbus had expected,

King Ferdinand the Catholic

A Spanish carrack from Columbus's *Carta*, 149.

. . . in thirty-three days time I reached the Indies with the fleet which the most illustrious King and Queen, our Sovereigns, gave to me, where I found very many islands thickly peopled, of all which I took possession without resistance, for their Highnesses by proclamation made and with the royal standard unfurled . . . I reached them in thirty-three days, and returned in twenty-eight . . . Christopher Columbus

Christopher Columbus had red hair and blue eyes; after Tobias Stimmer

From the earliest
woodcut of
American Indians,
1505

Columbus after De Bry

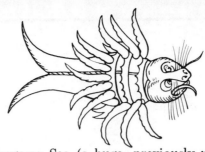

passing through the Sargasso Sea (a huge, previously unknown expanse of floating seaweed), encountering unexpected variations in the compass readings and, most worrisome of all, finding no sign of land. The sailors were increasingly restive and he had to use a combination of cajolery, deception (he faked the log so that they wouldn't know how far they had really gone) and maritime discipline to keep them in line. He offered a hefty reward for the person who first sighted land and, on the morning of October 12, a sailor claimed it, catching sight of what is probably one of the Bahamas.

With great pomp, Columbus claimed this and many other islands for Ferdinand and Isabella. He was received with great honor back in Spain, and prepared a much larger second voyage, to extend his great discoveries. Although Columbus was eager for riches and titles, he was more determined to discover what he had set out to find. He still had no firm evidence that he had reached Japan or China. In spite of illness, exhaustion and political misfortunes, he spent the rest of his life trying to confirm that he had landed somewhere near the east coast of Asia. On his fourth voyage (1502-4), when he discovered Central America, he thought that he was somewhere near the Straits of Malacca. At the same time that new explorers like Amerigo Vespucci were extending the discoveries and realizing that this was truly a New World, Columbus refused to admit it. He went to his death determined, as he was always determined, that he was right.

The early arms of Columbus

The arms of Pinzon, Columbus's pilot

Amerigo Vespucci

c. 1454-1512

Not everyone believed that Columbus had made it to Asia. His reputation as an explorer began to sink when the islands he discovered yielded little of the gold and spices he had promised. Europe was much more excited when Amerigo Vespucci, another Italian working in Spain, claimed to have found an entire new continent beyond the Atlantic.

Amerigo — hardly anyone called him Vespucci — was a friend of Columbus's and had helped outfit his third voyage. He had first come to Spain as an agent of the Medici bankers of Florence, then stayed on to do business on his own. At the turn of the century, he had the chance to take several voyages across the Atlantic. Though he was never the commander, he wrote letters to friends in Italy describing what he had seen of the coasts of South America. (Columbus reached the coast of Venezuela about the same time.) The continent was so large and so obviously un-Chinese that he had no doubts about calling it a "New World." A German mapmaker, who obviously agreed with him, put the name "America" on the section of coast Amerigo had described. As knowledge of the continent spread, that one impulsively chosen name spread with it.

The arms of Vespucci

Amerigo Vespucci

King Ferdinand and Queen Isabella

APARCTIAS

Mare glaciale.

100 200 210 220 230 240 250 260 210 280 290 300 310 320 330 340 3

90

John and Sebastian Cabot

John died c. 1498, Sebastian c. 1484 - 1557

Cabotto, Bagoto, Chiabotto, Savoto: this Italian name may have a dozen different forms, but they all mean "coaster." Anyone who carried one of these names had ancestors who once navigated ships around the Mediterranean, where sailors usually stayed as close to the coast as possible. Giovanni Caboto and his son Sebastian carried the name across strange waters to some very new coasts.

Giovanni was born in Genoa, possibly within a few years of Columbus, but had become a citizen of Venice by the 1470s and then travelled in the Near East. He later claimed to have made it to Mecca, where Arab merchants explained how many hands spices passed through on their way from Southeast Asia. It occurred to him that it might be easier to reach the spices by sailing west across the Atlantic.

He may have tried to sell his idea in Spain in 1492 and 1493. But Columbus had gotten there before him and in 1495 "John Cabot" was in England. In 1496 King Henry VII authorized him to explore for new lands across the North Atlantic. Raising the money for the voyage himself, Cabot had only one small ship, the *Matthew*, and about twenty men when he set sail from Bristol in May of 1497.

The North Atlantic Ocean is much narrower than the South and Cabot reached the coast of North America in a little over a month. He probably landed in Newfoundland, the first European there since the Vikings, and he may have explored as far south as New England. Though the coast was rocky and foggy, Cabot found fish and timber in abundance almost everywhere he went. King Henry rewarded him handsomely on his return to England and in 1498 he led a fleet of five ships back to the New World.

The arms of Bristol

But the North Atlantic is also much stormier than the South. One of Cabot's ships made it back to Ireland, but the other four were never heard of again. He had established the English claim to North America and English fishermen were soon working the American waters, but it was nearly a century before they tried to settle permanently there.

Cabot's son Sebastian may have taken part in the 1497 voyage. In the rest of a long and profitable career as expert on faroff places, he made only one other voyage of discovery. Starting as a mapmaker in England, he moved to Spain in 1512 and (now "Sebastian Cabota") became Pilot-Major in 1518. His expedition to the Moluccas in 1526 never made it beyond the Rio de la Plata in South America, but he remained a Spanish Pilot-Major until he returned to England in 1548. In the 1550s he was governor and superintendent of the expeditions the Muscovy Company sent into the Arctic. He seems to have been a genial, dignified and popular liar.

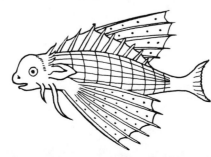

SPES · MEA · IN · DEO · EST.

EFFIGIES · SEBASTIANI CABOTI
ANGLIFIL II IOHANIS CABOTI VENE
TI MILITIS AVRATI PRIMI INMET
ORIS TERRÆ NOVA SVB HERICO VII ANGL
IÆ REGE

John Cabot from a lost painting, after James Herring, Bristol Art Museum

Ferdinand Magellan

c. 1480-1521

When Spain and Portugal agreed to divide their new discoveries between themselves in 1494, the Spanish thought that Columbus had reached the coast of Asia. Twenty-five years later it seemed that he had found a barrier to Asia instead. While the Portuguese controlled the route around the Cape of Good Hope, monopolizing the trade with the East, the Spanish would have to find a way over, through or around America to get there. In 1518, the soldier and mariner Ferdinand Magellan offered to lead an expedition to the Indies by sailing around the bottom of South America.

Magellan was a Portuguese himself, a member of the lower nobility, who had served with distinction in the Portuguese army in the Indies. But while he was later fighting in Morocco, he was accused of trading with the enemy and temporarily dropped from the service. Combining his knowledge of the Spice Islands with some recently published maps, he concluded that South America was an Asian peninsula and decided to sell his idea to the Spanish. His geography was just as faulty as Columbus's had been; the results of his voyage were almost as momentous.

The fleet of five ships left Spain on August 10, 1519. Except for a brief mutiny by Spanish sailors who resented having a Portuguese captain, the voyage across the Atlantic and down the east coast of South America was uneventful. The difficulties began when Magellan found what he was looking for. What we now call the Straits of Magellan are a 360-mile-long, cold, narrow, twisty series of passages among innumerable barren islands. After thirty-eight days in this labyrinth, the fleet was about to turn back when it finally reached what Magellan named the Pacific, or peaceful, Ocean.

It was not only peaceful, frequently windless, but also empty, and the crew suffered severe hunger as well as scurvy in the ninety-eight days it took to reach the first habitable island (probably Guam). But the islands were almost as dangerous as the open sea. Magellan and a number of his men were killed when they tried to intercede between warring factions in the Philippines. Only two of the ships made it on to the Moluccas, the "Spice Islands;" only one, loaded with cloves, left there for the fairly easy passage to Spain. Eighteen of the original 270 finally reached home, the first men to sail around the world.

1522 was a good year for Spain. At about the same time that the remnants of Magellan's fleet returned, reports began to arrive of Cortés's conquest of Mexico.

Arms of Ferdinand Magellan

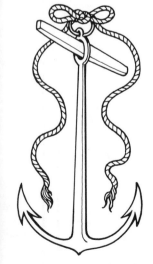

Magellan after Crispin de Passe

Hernán Cortés

c. 1485-1547

When he first sailed for Mexico in 1519, Cortés thought he might be on his way to a large island. The two Spanish expeditions that had left Cuba for Mexico since 1517 had found well-dressed Indians with stone buildings, intricate gold ornaments and highly trained armies, who spoke of a mighty empire somewhere inland. Even before the second expedition had returned, Diego Velázquez, the Governor of Cuba, chose Cortés to lead a third. His instructions were to explore and settle along the coast and look for gold, but Cortés began to prepare for a much more ambitious campaign. Worried that Cortés might try to set himself up on his own, Velázquez decided to relieve him of his command.

Cortés sailed away as if he had never heard the order. Even if it meant becoming an outlaw who would get no support from home, he was determined to be in charge. When his fleet landed near present-day Veracruz, he had his men incorporate a city and elect him Governor, responsible only to the King of Spain. Before his little army marched inland, he sank all their ships. They were in Mexico to stay.

Mexico, it turned out, was not an island but a continental empire as large and populous and in many ways as civilized as Spain. Impressive by Spanish colonial standards, Cortés's army of 700 was nothing to what the Aztec rulers of Mexico could command. But Cortés quickly learned his opponents' weaknesses. The Aztecs, who liked to tear the hearts out of their enemies, were hated by the other Mexicans; there were legends that a race of bearded white gods would come from the East; and the Aztecs had no experience of horses or guns.

The arms of Cortés

Cortés was a clever diplomat, a painstaking organizer and a decisive commander. Using persuasion when he could and force when he had to, he collected a large army of Indian allies as he marched overland to the Aztec capital of Tenochtitlán. There the Spaniards were greeted as gods; within a week they had taken the Emperor Montezuma prisoner and seemed in command of the Aztec state.

But religion divided them. The Spaniards hated the Aztec human sacrifices. When Cortés rushed back to Veracruz to stop an army Velázquez had sent, one of his lieutenants led a massacre of Aztec worshippers. The Aztecs rebelled and killed Montezuma; when the Spaniards fled Tenochtitlán at night, Cortés lost more than half his men. It took more than a year of savage fighting to recapture the city and destroy the Aztec empire.

The rest of Cortés's life was an anticlimax. He led expeditions to Honduras and Baja California, but he was less of an administrator than a soldier. The Emperor Charles never granted him the power he wanted in Mexico and he died embittered back in Spain.

Cortés after Christopher Weiditz, c. 1540

Vasco Núñez de Balboa

c. 1475-1519

Balboa

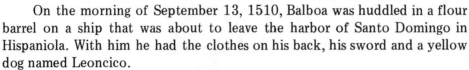

On the morning of September 13, 1510, Balboa was huddled in a flour barrel on a ship that was about to leave the harbor of Santo Domingo in Hispaniola. With him he had the clothes on his back, his sword and a yellow dog named Leoncico.

The ship, which was commanded by Martin Fernández de Enciso, was taking relief supplies to a settlement at Darién (near the modern border between Panama and Colombia). Much as he wanted to join the expedition, Balboa knew that his creditors would never let him out of town. After nine years in the New World, first as part of a pearl-hunting expedition, then as a planter on Santo Domingo, he was deeply in debt. Stowing away on an outgoing ship was his only chance to escape and start a new life.

He was caught, of course, and Enciso threatened to maroon him on a desert island. But before one was found, it was discovered that Balboa knew more about the Darién coast than anyone else on board. It soon turned out that he was also a much better leader of men than Enciso. When they reached the struggling Darién settlement, Balboa suggested moving it to a better location; the settlers then elected him one of their leaders, and soon Enciso returned to Santo Domingo.

Once in charge at Darién, Balboa began to strengthen the settlement and explore the area around it. Unlike many early settlers, he tried to deal peacefully with the neighboring Indians. Impressed by Spanish power and amused by the Spanish lust for gold, some of them offered to help Balboa conquer a rich tribe high in the mountains. In September, 1513, Balboa led 180 Spaniards and 800 Indians into some of the most impenetrable land on earth. After defeating the Indians of Quareca, they moved south over the crest of the mountains. Balboa was exploring alone with his dog Leoncico when, on September 27, 1513, he first caught sight of the Pacific Ocean.

He knew at once that he had found something important. He called his men together; they piled up stones with a cross on top to mark the site; their priest performed a *Te Deum* of thanksgiving. Then they marched for two days to the ocean itself, where Balboa and twenty-six of his men waded into the water with banners aloft to claim it for King Ferdinand. After exploring the coast and collecting gold and pearls, the expedition returned to Darién four months later.

There they learned that a new governor, the fearsome Pedrarias de Ávila, had been sent out from Spain. For the next four years, Pedrarias tried to push Balboa out of the way. In January, 1519, he had him tried on trumped up charges of treason, and illegally executed. No one knows what happened to Leoncico.

Arms of the New World

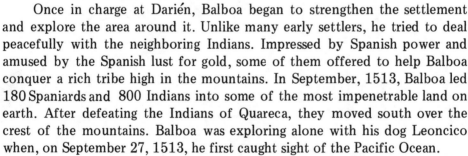

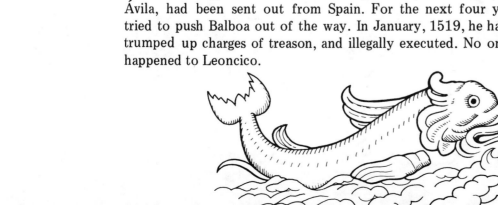

Álvar Núñez Cabeza de Vaca
c. 1490-1557

There were nearly 600 men and women in the expedition that Pánfilo de Narváez led from Spain in 1527. The number dropped very quickly. On the way to Florida, Narváez's five ships stopped at Hispaniola, where 140 deserted, and Cuba, where a hurricane wiped out sixty men and twenty horses. Once they reached Tampa Bay in April of 1528, Narváez split his party in two: 100 stayed on the ships while 300 headed up the coast on foot.

Cabeza de Vaca, who was treasurer and second-in-command of the expedition, was the only one to object. But staying with the ships seemed cowardly so he followed Narváez ashore in search of gold and friendly Indians. After three months' slogging through swamps and sand dunes they had found neither; they had lost all contact with their ships; a third of the party was seriously ill. In the late summer they ate their last horse, forged their spurs, stirrups and weapons into saws, axes and nails and built five barges. At the height of the hurricane season, they were going to try to sail from northern Florida to Mexico.

Arms of Cabeza de Vaca

Two of the barges, one commanded by Cabeza de Vaca, almost made it, reaching Galveston Island (in modern Texas) in November. But cold and hunger soon reduced the eighty survivors to fifteen. When Cabeza de Vaca fell ill himself, he lost touch with the other Spaniards and became a slave of the local Indians. He escaped in early 1530 and began trading among the Indians, exchanging the shells and mesquite beans of the coast for skins, flints or ochre of the interior; he probably got as far as Oklahoma.

Cabeza de Vaca

He might have spent the rest of his life among the Indians, but in late 1533 he came upon the three remaining survivors — two Spaniards and a Moorish slave — of the Narváez expedition. They met again the following summer and then travelled west together, working as medicine men among the tribes they encountered. Their healing was so successful that groups of Indians began to accompany them from one tribe to the next, taking what they wanted of their new hosts' possessions. After moving west through what is today Texas, New Mexico and Arizona, they turned south into Mexico proper and met a company of Spanish soldiers in March of 1536.

In his eight years in North America, Cabeza de Vaca had crossed two-thirds of the continent and adopted all the ways of the Indians except their religion. Grateful to be back among Christians, he found that he "couldn't stand to wear any clothes or to sleep anywhere except on the bare floor for a long time."

On returning to Spain, Cabeza de Vaca told of the rich cities of Quivira. He met the governor of Cuba and Florida, Hernando de Soto, who was enthralled by the stories.

SEAL OF THE GREAT UNIVERSITY OF SALAMANCA
where Balboa and De Soto had been students. If you study
hard and go to a good university, you too may become a
GREAT EXPLORER. The Space Age is just beginning, and
in just a very short time good students will be whizzing off
to Mars and far beyond, for sights never imagined by these
ancient heroes. To them, however, we owe much, for the
Spirit of Exploration came to America with them and is
the very spirit of our national character.

Balboa collecting
gold, after De Bry

Juan
Ponce de León

c. 1460-1521

In the spring of 1513, Ponce de León was sailing around the Bahamas searching for an island called Bimini when he came across a flat and pleasant-looking piece of land. It didn't seem to be what he was looking for, but he did his duty by going ashore and claiming what he thought was a large island in the name of King Ferdinand. Since it was near Easter *(Pascua Florida* in Spanish) and the land was so lushly wooded, he decided to call it *La Florida* (the flowery place). After discovering the Gulf Stream a little farther south, he explored the Florida coast and the Gulf of Mexico before returning home to Puerto Rico.

Some later Spanish historians claimed that Ponce de León had been trying to find a Fountain of Youth in Bimini. Earlier travelers had insisted that such a Fountain existed somewhere in Asia or Africa: bathing in it had enabled the legendary king Prester John to live to be 562. If the lands Columbus had just discovered really were on the outskirts of Asia, it was quite logical to think that there might be a Fountain of Youth in the vicinity.

But Ponce de León had an even better reason to go looking for a new island: he wanted to get away from the Columbus family. He had been one of the first Spaniards in the Western Hemisphere, arriving with Columbus on his second voyage in 1493. He rose steadily in the colonial administration, becoming governor of the province of Higuey on Hispaniola in 1504 and governor of the entire island of Puerto Rico — first he got the appointment, then he had to go conquer the island — in 1508. But when Columbus's son Diego came over in 1511 as Viceroy of all the lands his father had discovered, he brought his own men to serve under him, deposing Ponce de León and other incumbents. King Ferdinand tried to appease him with a charter to settle Bimini or any other lands Columbus had overlooked. He set out looking in early 1513.

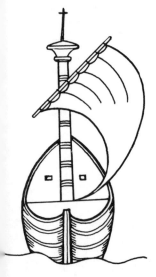

But even after he had found Florida, eight years passed before he could fulfill his wish to retire there. His services were still needed, if not always appreciated, in Puerto Rico; King Ferdinand died and the Spanish administration had to be reorganized, and Ponce de León had to settle his own affairs. In February, 1521 he finally set sail with two ships, 200 men and fifty horses. But the Florida Indians weren't at all friendly. They attacked the Spaniards when they tried to land near modern Fort Myers. Ponce de León was wounded by an arrow and died back in Cuba in July.

El Adelantado JUAN PONCE Des~
cubridor de la Florida.

Juan Ponce
de León
after J. B.
Verdusen

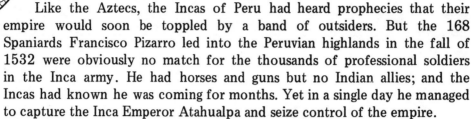

Francisco Pizarro

c. 1475-1541

Like the Aztecs, the Incas of Peru had heard prophecies that their empire would soon be toppled by a band of outsiders. But the 168 Spaniards Francisco Pizarro led into the Peruvian highlands in the fall of 1532 were obviously no match for the thousands of professional soldiers in the Inca army. He had horses and guns but no Indian allies; and the Incas had known he was coming for months. Yet in a single day he managed to capture the Inca Emperor Atahualpa and seize control of the empire.

He had luck on his side. Atahualpa had just defeated his brother Huáscar in a bloody civil war; if the Incas had been united, they might have stopped the Spaniards at the coast. And Atahualpa couldn't decide how to deal with them. When Pizarro had asked for a conference, Atahualpa had at first approached him with a large army, only to leave it behind and proceed with six thousand unarmed attendants. As he entered the city of Cajamarca where the Spaniards were encamped, their priest tried to convert the Inca to Christianity; he rejected it and they opened fire, slaughtering many of his companions and taking Atahualpa prisoner.

Pizarro knew how to take advantage of such luck; he had been in the New World since 1502, mostly helping others win fame and fortune. One of the first settlers in Darién, he had been Balboa's second-in-command on his trek to the Pacific; later he followed Pedrarias de Ávila when he moved his government across the Isthmus to Panama and he may have arrested Balboa for Pedrarias. Although illiterate, he was one of the leading citizens of Panama. In 1524, Pedrarias and others backed Pizarro and his friend Diego de Almagro in a search for the legendary Incas. Troublesome winds and currents had kept the Spaniards from sailing more than a few hundred miles down the coast before this, and it took Pizarro and Almagro four years of struggle (two expeditions with many reinforcements) to explore another 1000 miles. Pizarro returned briefly to Spain to win royal backing and recruit soldiers (including four of his half-brothers) for the conquest of Peru. He was named Governor of the new province; Almagro was to be only Commandant of a single city.

From a surviving fragment of Pizarro's flag

Almagro's arms

The difference between the partners almost undid the Spanish conquest. They captured the Inca capital of Cuzco in 1533. Almagro then led an expedition into Chile; on his return he crushed an Inca uprising, then seized Cuzco for himself. Pizarro, who had established a new capital, Lima, on the coast, moved against Almagro, who was killed in 1538. Three years later, Pizarro himself was assassinated by his followers in Lima.

Francisco Pizarro, Museo America, Madrid

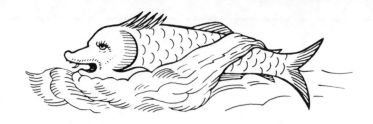

Hernando de Soto

c. 1500-1542

De Soto was the first European to meet the Inca Atahualpa. Sent by Pizarro to arrange a meeting between the Inca and the Spaniards, he rode ahead of his men right into the middle of the Inca's armed camp. He spurred his horse so close to Atahualpa that its hot breath rustled the Inca's sacred cap; Atahualpa remained totally still. De Soto began wheeling his horse around in a dashing display of riding skill and ended by charging straight at the Inca, says one source, bringing his mount to its knees directly in front of him; Atahualpa sentenced any of his chiefs who flinched to death. In spite of the Inca's calm, this show of courage by a single horseman weakened the Inca's resistance. The Spaniards captured Atahualpa the next day.

De Soto gained great wealth and was one of Pizarro's most trusted lieutenants, but still he was dissatisfied. He had already served faithfully in Panama and helped conquer Nicaragua; now he wanted some land for himself to rule. In 1536, he returned to Spain to seek this.

Arms of Xerez, birthplace of both De Soto and Balboa

Instead of giving him land in Central or South America, as he had hoped, the Council of the Indies made De Soto governor of Cuba, and offered him part of Florida to explore and conquer. Florida was largely unknown then (some still thought it was an island), but there were tales of gold and jewels somewhere in the interior. In May, 1539, de Soto landed with 650 men and women at Tampa Bay.

This time there was no great empire that could be defeated with a few bold strokes. As De Soto and his party moved east and north, they met small but well-armed and usually hostile Indian nations; for the next three years they were almost always fighting or ready to fight. After spending their first winter near modern Tallahassee, they headed north through Georgia in search of a rich and powerful queen. Finding pearls but no gold in her land, they crossed the Appalachian Mountains into what is today Tennessee, then moved south into Alabama and west to Mississippi.

After two years of marching and fighting, De Soto had lost half of his company when he first sighted the Mississippi River on May 8, 1541. Another year of exploring in Arkansas brought no sign of gold. De Soto had decided to abandon the expedition when he died of fever near present day Natchez in May 1542. His body was buried in the great river he had discovered.

Hernando de Soto after the 1728 edition of Herrera, *Historia General de los Hechos de los Castellanos*

Francisco
Vásquez de Coronado
c. 1510-1554

Viceroy Mendoza's arms

Coronado's arms

In 1540, Coronado was probably the most promising young man in Mexico. He had come over from Spain as secretary to Viceroy Mendoza, became a member of the Mexico City town council at twenty-eight and governor of the province of New Galicia a few months later. When Mendoza sent an army into the northern desert to find the seven cities of Cíbola, Coronado was obvious choice to lead it.

The rumor of seven cities of gold somewhere in the north had taken form from a mixture of old Spanish legends, stories Cabeza de Vaca had heard on his wanderings and the reports of the Franciscan friar Marcos de Niza. But all Coronado's army of 235 Spaniards and 1000 Indians (accompanied by hundreds of mules, cattle, sheep, goats and pigs) found at the end of a thousand-mile march was the Zuñi pueblo of Hawikuh (in modern New Mexico). The Zuñis, with their carefully irrigated fields and multi-storied adobe buildings, were far more sophisticated than the Indians Coronado has passed on his way, but they had no gold. The scouting expeditions he sent out were also disappointing: one reached the Grand Canyon; another crossed the Colorado River farther south and entered California; a fleet of support ships sailed up the Gulf of California into the Colorado River. Because they produced no gold, the Spaniards ignored these important discoveries.

After a winter in New Mexico, Coronado led part of his army to the northeast, where an Indian slave the Spaniards called "The Turk" insisted that there was a kingdom called Quivira, so rich that its king relaxed in a boat whose oarlocks were made of gold. They went as far as central Kansas before they realized that he had tricked them into taking him back to his home, a prosperous but very goldless Pawnee town. When they returned to New Mexico for the winter, it seemed to be Coronado's will alone that was keeping the disappointed army together. In the spring, he promised, the entire company would recross the plains and search for Quivira more thoroughly.

But in December, 1541, Coronado fell from his horse and was trampled by another. He almost died of head injuries, and his expedition came to a dispirited end. When his army straggled into Mexico City in the fall of 1542, it seemed that three years of preparation and exploration had been wasted. Coronado never completely recovered from his injuries and died when he was only forty-four.

His only failure was in not finding gold, but in his time that was enough. Although Coronado reached farther into North America than any Spaniard before him (and came within 500 miles of de Soto in the east), it was almost two centuries before any Spanish settlers followed his lead.

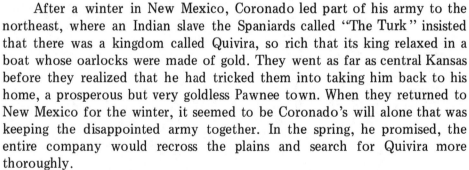

Probably the earliest picture of a buffalo, from Thevet's *Les Singularitez de la France Antarctique,* Antwerp, 1558

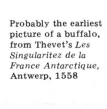

Juan Rodríguez Cabrillo

c. 1500-1543

The story of California came straight out of a book, a knightly romance published in 1510. It was a paradisiacal island "on the right hand of the Indies" where beautiful Queen Califia ruled over a country of beautiful black Amazons with lots of pearls and gold, and men were only allowed there one day a year to help perpetuate the race.

The hot and dusty island that Cortés's men found off the west coast of Mexico in 1535 was thought to be this story-book land, for they found pearls. Francisco de Ulloa, whose expedition of 1539 proved that the island was in fact a peninsula, named its southernmost tip the "Point of California." Although hot and dry, the new land was worth exploring: it might somewhere hold good land for settlement; it might veer west and lead to China.

Viceroy Antonio de Mendoza commissioned Juan Rodríguez Cabrillo to explore this coast in 1542. He had spent much of his life in the New World, for he had been just a boy when he came over from Spain with Pánfilo de Narváez for the conquest of Cuba; later he served Cortés in Mexico and Alvarado in Guatemala. He was rewarded with large estates in Guatemala, but in 1536 Alvarado asked him to oversee the construction of a fleet that would try to sail across the Pacific. When Alvarado died crushed by a horse and in debt in 1541, Cabrillo took over the fleet to recoup his investment. (He owned one of the vessels and had never been paid for his five years' work.)

Cabrillo and his three ships left the Mexican port of Navidad in June of 1542. In September he reached what he called San Diego harbor, and the land became more attractive, the Indians more prosperous and friendlier. By the end of the year Cabrillo had passed the Santa Barbara Channel islands, Monterey and San Francisco bays and the Russian River. Bad weather and leaky ships forced them to return for the winter to the Channel Islands, where Cabrillo died of an infected wound. The fleet sailed north again in the spring, but turned back at about the same point Cabrillo had already reached. Perhaps because he couldn't report in person about his discoveries, over two hundred years would pass before the Spanish tried to settle California.

From the statue on Point Loma, San Diego

Sir Francis Drake

c. 1540 - 1596

Drake's arms

Drake was engaged in a popular English pastime — plundering Spanish shipping in the Caribbean and Central America — when he crossed the Isthmus of Panama and caught sight of the Pacific Ocean. Resolving that he would be the first Englishman to sail there, he returned home and began to gather support for his expedition. Up to this point, he had been an independent entrepreneur, outfitting his own ships and risking his own capital, but his forays against the Spanish had served the national interest and made him a popular hero. In 1577, Queen Elizabeth I agreed to underwrite his exploration of the Pacific.

Drake's flagship the *Pelican* (later renamed the *Golden Hind*) led a fleet of five small ships, manned by 165 sailors, south from England, but he abandoned two of them off the coast of South America and then separated from the other two in the Straits of Magellan. Although the *Golden Hind* was adequate for one of Drake's principal activities, attacking Spanish ships and settlements along the coast, it was soon so full of loot that he moved on north to repair leaks.

On June 17, 1579, Drake landed north of San Francisco. Received as gods by the local Indians, the English named the land New Albion and claimed it for Queen Elizabeth.

The Golden Hind, crest of Sir Christopher Hatton

After sailing as far north as the present U.S.-Canadian border, Drake turned southwest and crossed the Pacific in two months. It took another year to make his way through the Indies, cross the Indian Ocean, round the Cape of Good Hope and return to England, where Queen Elizabeth knighted him on board the *Golden Hind*.

After a few years on shore, including a term as mayor of Plymouth, Drake returned to his true vocation, harrassing the Spanish. He led another expedition to the Caribbean, led the attack on the Great Armada and even took two fleets to attack the Spanish coast. By the time of his last voyage to the Caribbean, there was not much left to plunder. It may have been disappointment as much as dysentery that killed him near Portobello.

Sir Francis Drake after Hondius, 1580

Jacques Cartier

c. 1491-1557

On May 23, 1541 Jacques Cartier's fleet of five ships (manned by a strange mixture of noblemen and convicts) set sail from Saint-Malo to establish a French settlement in Canada. Cartier had already been there twice before. After a successful career as a commercial sea captain, sailing perhaps as far as Brazil and Newfoundland, he had been chosen by King François I to "discover new lands in the New World" for France. On his first voyage with two ships in 1534 he cruised the Gulf of St. Lawrence. This area was already familiar to French, English, Spanish and Portuguese fisherman, but Cartier was the first European to explore it systematically. Reaching the mouth of the St. Lawrence River, he thought he had found a possible passage through the North American continent.

The results of this voyage were so promising that the French king sent Cartier back in 1535 with provisions for a fifteen-month trip. This time he sailed down the St. Lawrence past Indian villages on the sites of modern Quebec and Montreal, until strong rapids made the river impassible. Returning to Quebec, the French spent their first winter among the Hurons, who showed them how to cure scurvy with the juice of the arborvitae tree, and entertained the Frenchmen with stories of a wealthy kingdom called Saguenay to the north.

Very little of these stories was true — the Indians were telling the French what they wanted to hear — but they were enough to inspire the colonizing voyage in 1541. It was the size of the expedition — this time Cartier was under the command of a soldier named Roberval, who would be Viceroy of New France — that alarmed the Emperor Charles V, who tried to stop the expedition. But it was Canada rather than the Emperor that defeated the French. Roberval failed to meet up with Cartier; Cartier's men spent a cold and miserable winter encamped near Quebec; then the Indians attacked and killed many of them. In the spring of 1542, Cartier decided to give up and go home.

Roberval passed Cartier on his way home, but he also gave up after a winter in the Canadian wilds. Cartier himself retired in honor to Saint-Malo. Sixty years passed before the French made another try at settling in Canada.

Jacques Cartier

The arms of Saint-Malo

Samuel de Champlain

c. 1567-1635

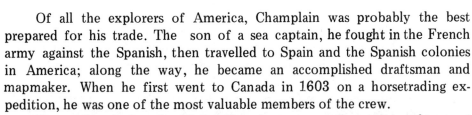

Of all the explorers of America, Champlain was probably the best prepared for his trade. The son of a sea captain, he fought in the French army against the Spanish, then travelled to Spain and the Spanish colonies in America; along the way, he became an accomplished draftsman and mapmaker. When he first went to Canada in 1603 on a horsetrading expedition, he was one of the most valuable members of the crew.

Fur traders had replaced the French crown as the main explorers of Canada, but it was only with the coming of Champlain that they settled in. He explored the St. Lawrence River, the coasts of Nova Scotia and Maine and founded the first permanent settlement at Quebec. This became the center of the French fur trade and Champlain became its leader. He made a policy of working peacefully with the local Huron Indians, even when this meant helping them in their wars with the neighboring Iroquois. On one campaign he discovered Lake Champlain in modern New York. Later he travelled by canoe with the Indians to the north and northwest as far as Lake Huron.

Maintaining support from France was almost as difficult as dealing with the Indians, the English and the weather in Canada, and Champlain was constantly returning home to seek support for his colony. He had crossed the Atlantic twenty-nine times when he died in Quebec in 1635.

Royal Arms of France

Henry Hudson
? -1611

In 1607, Henry Hudson, his son John and ten sailors took communion in a London church before departing on his first arctic voyage. In May, 1608, he attended the christening of his granddaughter Alice. These are the only two recorded events in his private life. He seemed to come out of nowhere, make four daring forays into one of the most inhospitable parts of the earth and then vanish again.

He must have already attained a high reputation as a navigator when the English Muscovy Company commissioned him to find a polar route to China in 1607. With the Muslims in control of the Near East, the Portuguese of the Cape of Good Hope and the Spanish of the Straits of Magellan, a passage through the Arctic Ocean offered the English their only chance for a direct route to the Orient.

On his first voyage, Hudson headed almost due north. His tiny ship *Hopewell* moved up the east coast of Greenland until it reached an impassable barrier of ice, turned east as far as the islands of Spitzbergen, then south and back to England. He sailed to nearly 80° north, destroying the theory that the climate might grow milder close to the North Pole, but discovering new fishing and whaling grounds for English fleets.

In 1608, the Muscovy Company sent Hudson and the *Hopewell* to search for a Northeast Passage along the upper coast of Russia. This time he managed to sail around the western shore of the Novaya Zemlya islands without finding a way through. It seems that he wanted to explore farther to the west on that voyage, but that his men refused to go on.

On his third voyage in 1609, the exact opposite occurred. While the Muscovy Company had stopped looking for a Northeast Passage, the Dutch East India Company was eager to send Hudson — with a larger ship, the *Half Moon* — back to Novaya Zemlya. But his crew mutinied on the way and he decided to look for a Northwest Passage through America instead. Sailing south from Newfoundland, he found a likely opening in New York Harbor and pushed far up what is now called the Hudson River before it became unnavigable.

The threat of Dutch competition led a group of English merchants to recruit Hudson back for another attempt to find a Northwest Passage. In 1610, while Dutch colonists were settling along the Hudson River, he piloted an English ship, the *Discovery*, through Hudson's Strait into Hudson's Bay (as they are now called). This seemed the most likely Passage of all, but ice and contrary currents made progress difficult and the *Discovery* was forced to winter at the south end of the Bay. In June of 1611, when the ship was free to sail again, the crew mutinied and set Hudson, his son John and several loyal sailors adrift in a small boat. In the next few years, other English ships sailed into the Bay to follow up on his discoveries, but Hudson was never seen again.

Muscovy Company Arms

Hudson's last voyage after the Hon. John Collier, The Tate Gallery, London

René-Robert Cavelier,
Sieur de La Salle

c. 1643-1687

The first French explorers in Canada had hoped that the St. Lawrence River might lead to the Chinese Empire. La Salle was more realistic and more ironic. Given a grant of land just beyond Montreal, where rapids make the river impassable, he simply declared his estate to be *La Chine* (China) and set out to found a French Empire in North America instead.

He had to rely on his own vision and the strength of his personality. He had lost his inheritance when he became a Jesuit novice; when he decided not to enter the priesthood, he emigrated to Montreal, where his older brother was a member of the Sulpician Order, which was attracting settlers with grants of land. But he was soon so enthralled by Indian reports of distant lakes and rivers that in 1669 he sold his land back to the Sulpicians to finance a trade and exploration expedition to the south. Along the way he may have discovered the Ohio River, and he learned enough about western geography and the fur trade to offer startling new plans to the Comte de Frontenac, governor-general of New France. He proposed to expand French rule from the Great Lakes to the Mississippi Valley, making alliances with local Indian tribes and building forts in strategic locations.

La Salle's plans won support from both King Louis XIV and the governor-general, but his progress was slow. He was opposed by the established fur traders and Jesuit missionaries, and had to raise his own capital from the fur trade and then lead very small expeditions into the hostile wilderness. Forts he built near Lakes Erie and Michigan were destroyed by Indians or French deserters; the ship he had launched on Lake Erie was lost in a storm. But he gradually extended his series of forts into modern Illinois and began to explore the upper Mississippi. In 1682, he led a tiny party downstream to the mouth of the Mississippi and claimed all of "Louisiana" (the watershed of the Mississippi River and its tributaries) for France.

But when he returned to Quebec, La Salle found that the new governor-general had taken away his powers. La Salle had to travel to France to be reinstated by the king; there he came up with the idea of settling the Mississippi from the south. But the expedition there turned out to be a disaster. The captain of the fleet missed the Mississippi, dropped La Salle and his men in what is now Texas and sailed away. The party of 230 dwindled to forty-seven as La Salle made three attempts to march overland to the Mississippi. Returning from the third try, he was shot dead by some of his own men.

The arms of La Salle

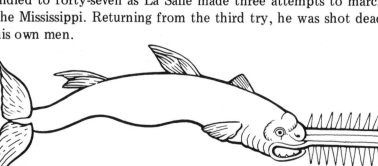

DÉCOUVERTE DU COURS DU MISSISSIPI ET DE LA LOUISIANE. 1699.

The discovery of the Mississippi River, after La Salle's death

Champlain in action, 1609, a self-portrait in *Les Voyages*, 161

Fathers Marquette and Jolliet in New France

The Jesuit Banner

Jacques Marquette and Louis Jolliet

Marquette c. 1637-1675 Jolliet c. 1645-1700

While he was still quite young, Marquette determined to become a missionary in newly discovered lands; he even had an ambition to become a martyr, like his hero St. Francis Xavier, alone and unaided in a foreign wilderness. Born into a family long prominent as merchants and public servants, he entered a Jesuit school when he was nine, and was a novitiate when he was seventeen. He began teaching Latin two years later and worked in a number of Jesuit schools in France during the next decade. His superiors felt that his passion for exotic places needed to be tempered with time.

Even after he arrived in Canada in 1666, Marquette had to bide his time in the settled areas around Quebec and Montreal while he learned Indian languages and demonstrated his zeal and stamina. When he was finally sent to work among the Indians along the shores of Lakes Superior and Michigan — the farthest Jesuit outposts in New France at the time — he yearned to go even farther, among the Illinois who lived to the south. But he had been put off by his superiors so often that he was taken by surprise when Louis Jolliet arrived at his mission in late 1672 and announced that the two of them had been selected to find the Mississippi River, which they had heard of from the Indians.

Jolliet had been born near Quebec and grown up with the Huron Indians. Intelligent and musically talented, he had studied at a Jesuit school and planned to enter the priesthood himself. But he left school in 1667 and followed his brother Adrien into the fur trade instead. In the next five years he travelled as far as the western end of Lake Superior. Then the Intendant of New France commissioned him to find the Mississippi.

Jolliet and his five companions sought furs, while Marquette sought souls, and a passage through North America. The little party canoed across Lake Michigan into the Fox River, portaged to the Wisconsin River, then paddled to the Mississippi. In exactly two months, they travelled 1700 miles, as far as the Arkansas, before they decided to turn back in order to avoid the Spanish they expected to find on the Gulf coast.

Though the short expedition was a great success, the French government decided to keep the discovery secret. Marquette returned to found a mission among the Illinois a year later and died among his flock in 1675. Jolliet went on to explore Hudson Bay and Labrador and became a royal hydrographer of New France shortly before his death.

Captain James Cook

1728-1779

Cook's posthumous arms

Captain Cook

Most of the great explorers achieved their fame by finding something that many others had been seeking (Da Gama) or by discovering some place that no one had ever imagined existed (Columbus). Cook's greatest achievement came in not finding places other people were convinced were there. Along the way, he made the most meticulous investigation anyone had ever done of the largest single portion of the earth — the Pacific Ocean. As sailor, geographer, cartographer, diplomat, administrator and leader of men, he was probably more competent than any explorer before him.

He had to be. The son of a Scottish farm laborer, he depended on his own ability to make his way in the world. After a short apprenticeship to a grocer, he went to work as a merchant sailor and quickly rose to officer's rank. In 1755, he joined the Royal Navy, where promotion was much slower, but his private study of navigation, mathematics and cartography brought him opportunities to demonstrate his skill. The charts he made of the St. Lawrence River during the Seven Years War and of Labrador and Newfoundland after the war were some of the most complete and exact ever made.

In 1768, the Royal Society sent Cook and a team of scientists to make astronomical and geographical observations in the South Pacific. In particular, he was supposed to locate "Terra Australis," the great southern continent which many geographers insisted must lie south of the Straits of Magellan. Although he found no sign of such a place on either his first voyage, which lasted until 1771, or his second, from 1772 to 1775, he made a thorough exploration of New Zealand, the west coast of Australia and many of the major island groups of the Pacific. On his third voyage, which concentrated on the North Pacific between 1776 and 1779, he proved that a "Northwest Passage" around North America was impossible, but carefully investigated the west coast to the Bering Sea, discovering the Hawaiian Islands on his way.

Cook was the most thoughtful of captains, the first to systematically use fresh fruits and vegetables to combat scurvy among his crews, which thereafter spared many thousands of sailors' lives and reduced the terror of the seas. He was one of the first to insist that his men treat the natives they encountered with respect; it was a tragic irony that he was killed in a squabble with the native Hawaiians.

Captain Cook after John Webber,
National Art Gallery, Wellington
Mrs. Cook didn't like this portrait.